LUDWIG VAN BEETHOVEN

The Classic Romantic

THE HISTORY HOUR

CONTENTS

INTRODUCTION

ꙮ

Ludwig van Beethoven (1770-1827) was born in the small German city of Bonn in the Electorate of Cologne, part of the Holy Roman Empire on December 16, 1770. As a young man, he was recognized for his remarkable talent, although he was always compared unfavorably to his contemporary, Wolfgang Amadeus Mozart (1756-91), who took up all the oxygen in the musical world, leaving Beethoven to appear as a second-rate child prodigy. Even so, his work ethic, which was formidable, allowed him to eventually surpass Mozart's reputation, partly because he outlived Mozart, and went on to become the great composer of his day. His style, incomparable to any of the composers who came after him, has remained the standard of greatness never achieved by anyone else. He wrote only one opera, Fidelio, but wrote nine symphonies (as compared to the 104 by Haydn and the 44 by Mozart), which set the standard for Romantic composers. All those who came after him, from Schubert to Brahms, Mendelssohn, Schumann, and the two great late Romantic symphonists Mahler and Bruckner, compared themselves unfavorably to Beethoven.

⚜

Beethoven was a pianist and a violist, and he excelled in the fields of the string quartet, the piano sonata, and the concerto, writing the greatest works of all time in these areas as well. His late string quartets and the work he called the "***Grosse Fugue***" are widely considered the greatest works in this medium, and his piano sonatas namely the "***Moonlight***," "***Hammerklavier***," and the "***Pathetique***" are considered the finest works in this medium as well. His Violin Concerto and his piano concertos are among the most sophisticated and beautiful in all of classical music.

⚜

Stylistically, his early work is derivative of the other great Classical composers, Haydn and Mozart, but he also set the parameters for the Romantic style in his great symphonies and concertos, including the Eroica (Symphony #3), the Pastorale (#6), and the great Choral Symphony (#9). His abilities in vocal music are less brilliant, partly because of the difficulty he had setting text, despite his opera Fidelio and his great mass, the Missa Solemnis. The melody for the final movement of the "***Choral***" (Ninth) Symphony, from which is taken the famous and beautiful "***Ode to Joy***" is one of the best-known pieces of music ever written.

Beethoven created his work out of small musical motifs, which gave his music an integrity that no composer has ever matched. He would develop melodies and longer lines out of small musical germs of a few notes and develop them into massive sweeping melodies like the tune from the opening movement of the Pastorale Symphony (#6) or the "***Ode to Joy***." He created huge architectural structures from these disparate parts for his music based on the classical form par excellence, the sonata form.

Beethoven's life was fraught with brushes with greatness; he had little respect for those who did not work for their fame. He regularly insulted kings and emperors, and his anger with Napoleon when he crowned himself Emperor of France is legendary. He tore up the title page of his symphony that he was going to call "***Bonaparte***," but retitled it to "***Eroica***" with the subtitle "***to the memory of a great man***." Similarly, he scorned the fawning behavior of the great author Johann von Goethe, who courted the wealthy and the influential.

He was in love many times, and he loved profoundly but never married anyone; his face was scarred with smallpox, and he was not a man of cleanliness. In many ways, he was a confirmed bachelor from an early age. He took care of his relatives, including his mother and his nephew, but never had a family of his own. Probably the oddest and the biggest impediment to his marriage and happiness is the fact that early on in his career, he began to go deaf. By the time he was thirty years old, he was totally deaf, and although he devised many innovative ways to communicate and even to hear in a fashion, this would be a huge problem for him to live a normal life.

🙌

Although Beethoven died as a relatively young man (at fifty-six), he has left a mark on Classical music that is still felt by composers today, and his music is the center of both of the European styles of Classical and Romantic music.

❧ II ❧
BEETHOVEN'S FAMILY

"A great poet is the most precious jewel of a nation."

— LUDWIG VAN BEETHOVEN

❧

The Beethoven name, as the '*van*' suggests, is not of German origin. Beethoven's great-grandfather, Louis, moved from Malines in modern-day Belgium in the 1732 to Liège, and a year later was hired at the court of the Elector of Cologne in Bonn and attained the position of Kapellmeister in 1761. He was also a wine trader to supplement his income.

❧

Ludwig also became the Kapellmeister, and his son Johann, Beethoven's father, was a singer at the court. Sadly,

Beethoven's father did not possess the qualities necessary to rise in the musical world. Being a talented singer, he began his career as a treble in the court choir, and when his voice broke, he became a notable tenor. As a well-trained musician, he was competent in many areas of music and gave lessons to young people in the town, including his own son, Ludwig.

※

The Beethoven family lived at 515 Bonngasse Straße in Bonn. At the time of Beethoven's birth, Johann van Beethoven was a singer who worked for the Elector of Cologne; his mother, Maria Magdalena Keverich, was the daughter of the chief cook in the elector's household. She had already been married and was widowed before she married Johann. Johann's father, the Kapellmeister of the court, was a well-respected and proud man who objected to the marriage of this son to this *"lowly kitchen maid"* (as he called her), from whom he expected great things.

※

Nevertheless, they were married in a simple Roman Catholic ceremony, and she bore Johann a son in April 1769, whom they named Ludwig (Maria); he died when he was only six days old. One of Beethoven's more disturbing memories is being taken to the grave of his namesake brother each Sunday to contemplate the nature of mortality. Only a short time after the death of this son, Beethoven's mother gave birth to another son whom they also named Ludwig van Beethoven (this is the famous composer), named after Beethoven's distinguished grandfather, the Kapellmeister of the Elector of Cologne.

Beethoven had six siblings, including the Ludwig Maria Beethoven who predeceased him - a total of four brothers and two sisters - and he took it upon himself to support those who survived infancy after his mother died and his father became an uncontrollable drunkard. His sister, Anna Maria, lived for only four days, and his other sister, Margareth, died when she was one and a half years old, shortly after the death of her mother. His youngest brother, Franz Georg, died at two and a half. Only his brothers, Caspar and Johann, survived into adulthood.

Beethoven's mother died in 1787 when he was studying in Vienna, trying to make a name for himself. His father wrote him a letter to tell him that she was gravely ill with consumption, and so he returned to be with her at her deathbed. Following this, Beethoven returned to Vienna to continue his studies, and a few years later in 1792, his father died broke and destitute. Beethoven continued to support his younger brothers who survived until they were married. This sort of family loyalty was a trademark of Beethoven. He was loyal to any fault with his friends, his family, and his nephew Karl, the son of Carl who was known to be a dissolute fool and was treated with kid gloves by Beethoven even after the ingrate renounced Beethoven. This loyalty to the dissolute fop that Karl turned out to be is difficult to reconcile with a man with such high standards for himself; he was known to have disapproved of Karl's mother Johanna, who was left a widow when Beethoven's brother, Carl, died. The boy was only ten years old, and Beethoven went to court to get full custody of the youth. This led to a protracted legal battle between the mother and the composer, with Karl in the middle, having to give evidence of his mother's unfitness.

⚜

This clearly hurt the young man who was naturally fond of his mother. Nevertheless, Beethoven did eventually get sole custody of the youth when he was fourteen and forbade him from seeing his mother. Despite this proscription, he frequently ran away to see her against Beethoven's wishes.

⚜

Beethoven decided that Karl would be a musician and asked his student, Carl Czerny, the greatest pedagogue in the nineteenth century, to teach him. Beethoven refused to believe Czerny when he declared that the boy had no musical talent. Instead, he forced him to study music, leading to a rift between the two. Karl decided to study philology and eventually settled with a career in the military, which caused Beethoven a great deal of angst. On several occasions, Karl attempted suicide, and this is widely believed because of the pressure exerted on him by the opinionated and passionate Beethoven. Finally, in 1826, Karl made a serious attempt at suicide by shooting himself in the temple. When found, he asked to be taken to his mother's house rather than the home of his uncle, and this personal tragedy is often cited as the reason for Beethoven's health to declined to such an extent that he died the following year. Karl, who had been estranged from his uncle for more than a year returned to take part in the funeral rites for the great composer and was the sole heir to Beethoven's considerable fortune, living comfortably for the rest of his life, marrying and bearing four children, one of whom he named Ludwig.

❧ III ❧

EARLY LIFE IN BONN

"Music comes to me more readily than words."

— LUDWIG VAN BEETHOVEN

༺༒༻

As we have noted, Ludwig van Beethoven was born into a world of German musicians, and the subject of most interest at the time was Wolfgang Amadeus Mozart, the child prodigy who was astonishing all of Europe. Mozart had appeared at about 1761 touring as a child prodigy (the German word was "***Wunderkind***") throughout the royal houses of Europe. He had made a favorable impression on nearly everyone, and the concept of the child prodigy was seized upon by Johann van Beethoven who, by most accounts, was a drunkard and abusive father to young Ludwig.

Johann taught him the rudiments of music and, according to Beethoven, forced him to play later at night after he came home drunk from the taverns, making him stand on a stepstool and play. He reportedly beat him for the least hesitation. Either because of or despite this treatment, Beethoven developed into a phenomenal harpsichord (and later piano) player. He also learned the basics of violin and viola. At the time, it was standard musical pedagogy to learn all the instruments of the baroque orchestra, so the fact that Beethoven was adept at many instruments was not particularly noteworthy.

To capitalize on the fad of the Wunderkind, Johann van Beethoven announced a concert on March 26, 1778. Though Beethoven was born in 1772 (which Beethoven himself believed for many years), he presented himself as somewhat more aged than usual six-year-old and as an eight-year-old. The effort did not work, but it did attract the interest of the court organist, Gottlob Neefe (1748-98), a distinguished musician and organist.

In the meantime, Beethoven was studying at a Latin grade school named Tirocinium, and according to the memories of his classmates, he struggled with spelling and grammar. All of his life, Beethoven had trouble with these things, and many Beethoven scholars speculate that he may have suffered from a mild form of dyslexia. He withdrew from this school at age ten to study music full-time with Neefe and never went to school again. Nevertheless, Beethoven sought out teachers and worked extremely hard all of his life.

In 1781, Gottlob Neefe (1848-98), who was court organist, took Beethoven on as a student and recognized his remarkable talents, giving him the opportunity to perform at an early stage. Making him assistant organist, he gave Beethoven the challenge to play in church services while he was away with the traveling opera, which gave him his other employment. Neefe also gave Beethoven the chance to learn the basics of composition, and Beethoven's first published composition was at the age of twelve. This composition was a set of piano variations on a theme by an obscure classical composer named Dressler. Although this work is now lost, his next work was three harpsichord sonatas written in 1783 when Beethoven had not yet turned 13. He dedicated this work to Max-Friedrich, the Elector of Cologne. Dedicating a piece to a potential patron was common practice at the time, but this particular dedication seemed to have fallen on deaf ears, as the family's financial situation did not change.

By 1784, Johann van Beethoven was no longer able to support his family and so Beethoven, at thirteen, requested the appointment as Assistant Court Organist at an annual salary of one hundred and fifty florins, a good wage, which helped his family a great deal. Beethoven also played viola in the Imperial Court Orchestra supported by the Elector Spiritual of Cologne, and Archbishop of Muenster, Maximilian Franz (1756-1801), the youngest son of Maria Theresa, Empress of Austria and brother of Emperor Joseph II.

One of the well-kept secrets of the Classical period was the music of baroque composer, Johann Sebastian Bach. Bach had died in 1750, revered as the most celebrated organist to have ever lived, but wholly forgotten as a composer by all except organists. Interestingly, many of his sons were composers, and Carl Philip Emmanuel Bach, the principal composer in the court of Frederick the Great of Prussia, made Bach's music available to organists. Neefe taught this music to Beethoven, who was fascinated by the contrapuntal style of the older composer, counterpoint, or the combining of many melodies together in a musical tapestry of sound, was very rare at this time, and the simple melody with accompaniment was the popular style.

In 1791, Maximilian Franz took the court orchestra to his summer palace at Mergentheim, a trip along the Rhine and Main Rivers. Beethoven was appointed kitchen scullion while on the riverboat and was presented with a scroll commemorating this task. Oddly, Beethoven kept this until his death. Beethoven enjoyed the patronage of Maximilian Franz for many years, ending in 1794 only when the invading Napoleonic army dissolved his court. Maximilian fled to Vienna and continued to remain in contact with Beethoven until his death in 1801. Beethoven was planning on dedicating his First Symphony to the former Elector, but after his death, he changed the dedication to Baron Gottfried von Swieten, who was a composer of some note as well as a diplomat and who became a patron of Beethoven.

❧ IV ❧

EARLY YEARS IN VIENNA

"I will seize fate by the throat; it shall certainly never wholly overcome me."

— LUDWIG VAN BEETHOVEN

❦

Beethoven was sent to Vienna in 1787, supported by the Elector Spiritual of Cologne and Archbishop of Muenster, Maximilian Franz, to develop what the Elector believed was a unique musical talent. Vienna at that time was the unquestioned center of European music. Not only was the great composer Mozart was working there with great success, producing operas like The Marriage of Figaro and Cosi fan tutte, but he was also organizing concerts of his own music, sonatas, concertos, and symphonies at great speed. Similarly, Franz Joseph Haydn (1732-1809), who had been the director of music at Esterhaza in Hungary, spent his summers in Vienna, performing to huge crowds and attracting international attention through his published music for piano, string quartet, baryton trio, and the newly standardized group of instruments referred to as the symphony. Joseph Haydn's brother, Michael Haydn (1737-1806), was nearly as famous as his older brother and was in the same media of the symphony, the concerto, and other forms of classical ensembles. Johann Georg Albrechtsberger (1736-1809) was popular, producing baroque style contrapuntal music that was both popular and viewed as somewhat complicated and out of date. The hugely popular, Carl Ditters von Dittersdorf (1739-99), a pedantic and dull composer who nevertheless enjoyed phenomenal popularity in Vienna, was one of the most famous composers of the era. His symphonies were influential in establishing what we consider the Classical style, and his Singspiels (a German form of Classical opera) included Doktor und Apotheker (1786), the most popular event of that year. The noted woman composer, Marianna Martines (1744-1812), was active and very popular with her masses, oratorios, piano music, and for her vocal performance abilities. Although being a woman composer at the time was considered an oddity, Martines managed to overcome this obstacle and influenced many other composers. Antonio Casimir Cartellieri (1772-1807) was a Polish-born composer who enjoyed great popularity writing divertimentos, a popular dance-style of music, although his reputation was tarnished after his death. Cartellieri was a great proponent of the young Beethoven, premiering Eroica Symphony among his other works.

৩৩

Many other composers of Italian and French origin had

settled in the relative stability of Vienna due to the ongoing wars in Italy and the turmoil of the beginnings of the French Revolution in Paris.

ॐ

The premiere musical form in Paris at that time was known as the Sinfonia Concertante, a sort of precursor to the Classical symphony. Composers such as Kozeluch, Gossec, and Gresnick excelled in this form, and many of them moved from Paris to Vienna in the tumultuous period of the French Revolution (1789-99).

ॐ

Italian composers like Antonio Salieri, who became the court composer from 1774 to 1792, were making great strides there given the proximity of Tuscany and the popularity of Italian opera. Even German-speaking composers often wrote their operas in Italian.

ॐ

Not only was the court a hotbed of creativity and musical experimentation, but thanks to innovators like Mozart, public concerts of large works including piano and violin concertos, symphonies, and other large-scale works were becoming popular. With a population of more than two hundred thousand, Vienna was one of the largest cities in Europe. It also had extensive development of the land, thanks to many great architects in the early eighteenth century like Johann Bernhard Fischer von Erlach and Johann Lukas von Hildebrandt who built many new palais-style castles in the outskirts of Vienna including the Palais Liechtenstein, the

Palais Modena, the famous Schönbrunn Palace, the Palais Schwarzenberg, and the Belvedere (the garden palais of Prince Eugene of Savoy).

◈

Starting in 1783, Vienna was ruled by the wise and modern Emperor, Joseph II, who set about modernizing the city administration and giving the city a stability that was the envy of Europe. This stability attracted many composers to the city, and the city had been prominent in music history principally because of this intensely creative period in history. There was a great deal of opportunity for advancement and creative collaboration in Vienna.

❧ V ☙

BEETHOVEN'S TEACHERS

"Tones sound, and roar and storm about me until I have set them down in notes."

— LUDWIG VAN BEETHOVEN

❧❦❧

When Beethoven first arrived in Vienna, he sought out a career as a performer. He studied counterpoint to improve his composition skills and took violin lessons from the great violinist Ignaz Schuppanzigh but focused on his piano performance.

❧❦❧

As a composer, Beethoven was never one to follow trends; although his early music sounds a great deal like the popular composers of his day, Haydn and Mozart, it is clear that he strove to say something more profound. To this end, he traveled as soon as he could to Vienna, the seat of the so-called Viennese School, in which he would become its most important composer.

⊙⊱⊰⊙

Mozart was the most brilliant and facile composer ever to have lived. Nineteenth-century biographer Otto Jahn wrote about the one meeting between the two great composers:

> *Beethoven made his appearance in Vienna as a youthful musician of promise in the spring of 1787 but was only able to remain there for a short time; he was introduced to Mozart and played to him at his request. Mozart, considering the piece he performed to be a studied show-piece, was somewhat cold in his expressions of admiration. Beethoven, noticing this, begged for a theme for improvisation, and inspired by the presence of the master he revered so highly, he played in such a manner as gradually to engross Mozart's whole attention; turning quietly to the bystanders, he said emphatically, "Mark that young man; he will make himself a name in the world!"*

⊙⊱⊰⊙

However, it was about this time that Beethoven's mother died, and he left before Mozart was able to teach him.

⊙⊱⊰⊙

Franz Joseph Haydn was traveling the world in a series of concerts organized by Johann Peter Salomon, a great impresario who engineered the unparalleled success of Haydn in London England. On his way there, Haydn stopped in Bonn, where Beethoven was visiting, and Beethoven asked to be his student. Haydn had been the composer in residence at the highest court in the German-speaking world, Esterhaza, and agreed to take Beethoven on as a student of the art of counterpoint (the blending of multiple melodies into a single unified whole).

৩ॐ৩

Beethoven, ever the diligent student, worked harder than Haydn expected or wanted. Haydn, for his part, was getting old and was enormously busy with commissions for England and appeared not to have been particularly diligent as a teacher. Beginning lessons in 1792, Beethoven worked very hard, and Haydn was just not up for this sort of a student. He set him to work on the lessons codified by Johann J. Fux in his influential counterpoint textbook called Gradus ad Parnassum. This book had been the standard for counterpoint for many years, and Beethoven felt that he could have taught himself this. There are many stories of Beethoven catching Haydn being lazy and missing mistakes that he deliberately wrote in his assignments. Haydn was frustrated by this sort of criticism, and Beethoven made fast progress under Haydn but did not make friends with him. In 1795, Beethoven premiered his three Lichnowsky Trios with Haydn as a guest of honor. Haydn was tired and fell asleep during the concert. Beethoven asked him afterward what he had thought of the trios, and when Haydn suggested that the third trio needed some work before it was sent for publication, Beethoven was apparently insulted.

Nevertheless, he did revise the work, and it is regarded as his greatest trio today. As evidence that Beethoven was not forever insulted, he dedicated his next set of trios to his teacher. Nevertheless, when questioned later, Beethoven declared that he had *"never learned anything from Haydn."* Beethoven was given to hyperbole and fostered the idea that he was self-taught, and this is believed to be the reason for his claim.

In 1793, Beethoven sought out noted teacher Johann Schenk (1753-1836) with whom he had informal lessons. According to Schenk, he secretly and for free corrected the lessons that Haydn had overlooked. Similarly, Beethoven sought out Antonio Salieri who was considered a great and kind teacher, composer, and performer, but subsequently, he has become inextricably associated with the death of Mozart. This myth is false and was invented by the Russian writer Pushkin, but it has dogged his reputation ever since. As a teacher, Salieri was probably the best that Beethoven ever had and was likely the most influential on the future career of Beethoven. He also taught Schubert, who was the other great Viennese composer but who, although, lived for a time only a few blocks away from Beethoven, never met him. This was because, in the early 19th century, Beethoven had become the premier Viennese composer and Schubert, who was gay and was ostracized by the Viennese upper class.

During this period after Haydn had departed Vienna,

Beethoven sought out Johann Georg Albrechtsberger to give him lessons in counterpoint. He had been paid by his benefactor, the Elector of Bonn Maximilian Franz, but when Haydn departed, he stopped the payments. Nevertheless, he allowed Beethoven to stay in Vienna "***until recalled***." (He was never recalled.) According to contemporary reports, Beethoven was a very hard-working student who was also very headstrong and unwilling to accept anything at face value.

෴

Consequently, he had to experience failure himself and learned his lessons the hard way. Albrechtsberger worked with Beethoven for about a year and a half during which time he advanced very quickly. From 1795, Beethoven began to develop his own style of composition, strongly influenced by the counterpoint lessons he had received from Albrechtsberger.

❧ VI ❧
BEETHOVEN'S PATRONS

"Nothing is more intolerable than to have to admit to yourself your own errors."

— LUDWIG VAN BEETHOVEN

❧

Throughout his career, Beethoven sought patrons. A patron is a wealthy person, usually a nobleman, who gave money to an artist so that the artist could pursue his or her craft. In the eighteenth century, nearly every composer was patronized either by a wealthy donor or by the church. This was the case with Johann Sebastian Bach who worked his entire career for the Lutheran Church. Similarly, Jean-Baptiste Lully worked for Louis XIV, and many other composers.

❧

Closer to home, there were many musicians and composers in particular who received patronage in Vienna and the greater German-speaking world. Haydn was patronized by the Counts Esterhazy, among the wealthiest noblemen in Austria, while the Emperor Joseph II himself patronized Salieri. Carl Philipp Emanuel Bach, the eldest son of Johann Sebastian Bach, was the court composer to Frederick the Great of Prussia, who was himself a flute player and composer. Even Mozart, who is often regarded as the freelance musician that started the "starving artist" aesthetic, received some patronage from the royal court as a composer of dance music, and earlier, from the court in Salzburg, his hometown. He was also patronized at various times for smaller jobs by noblemen of the Austrian court.

❧

With the French Revolution though, patronage in France very nearly came to an end. Of course, there were those who continued to provide sustenance to composers, but Napoleon and the revolutionaries dismantled the royal patronage system and replaced with nothing. Similarly, when Napoleon's government began to export their own brand of democracy and revolution to the other countries of Europe, patronage began to suffer significantly. Despite Beethoven's oft-quoted support for democracy and citizens' rights, he was always in search of patronage.

❧

Beethoven found a good deal of patronage and made an excellent living under the patronage system. Beethoven had a patron in Bonn too. Count Waldstein, the dedicatee of the Waldstein Sonata Op. 53, was his first great patron while in

Bonn. When he moved to Vienna in November 1792, Beethoven came with a letter of introduction from Count Waldstein, his Bonn patron, to Prince Karl Lichnowsky, one of Vienna's foremost patrons of the arts. The relationship was slow to get going, but by 1796, Lichnowsky traveled to Prague, taking Beethoven with him. But 1800, Lichnowsky was providing Beethoven with an annual allowance of 600 florins under the condition that he would continue to receive this until he got a regular position as a musician (which actually never happened). Beethoven, being Beethoven, ended this relationship when he had an angry argument with Lichnowsky. Apparently, Beethoven was staying at Lichnowsky's country estate and refused to perform for some visiting French officers. According to witnesses, when Beethoven got home, he smashed a bust of Lichnowsky. Nevertheless, he dedicated seven of his compositions to Lichnowsky, including the three piano trios, op. 1 from 1793, the Nine Piano Variations on 'Quant'è più bello' from Giovanni Paisiello's opera La Molinara (1795), the Pathétique Sonata, op 13 (1798), the op 26 Piano Sonata (1801), and his Second Symphony (1802).

His greatest patron was the youngest son of Emperor Leopold II, a man named Archduke Rudolf. He was an excellent musician himself, a pianist and a composer of some ability, and he appreciated Beethoven's gifts in part because he was Beethoven's only composition student. He was also a sickly man, an epileptic who was often unwell.

It was in 1809 that he began his patronage in earnest. It was because Beethoven, then a household name in Vienna, had just accepted a position in Westphalia as Kapellmeister at the court in Kassel under King Jerome of Westphalia, the brother of Napoleon. This bothered Archduke Rudolf who persuaded a group of Viennese noblemen to band together to offer an annuity to Beethoven to stay in Vienna. He arranged for Prince Lobkowitz to provide an annuity of seven hundred florins and Prince Kinsky to promise Beethoven One thousand eight hundred florins, while he contributed fifteen hundred florins so that he did not accept the position in Kassel and remain in Vienna as a resident for the rest of his life. Beethoven naturally agreed to this arrangement.

૭૪ૐ

As luck would have it, nothing is forever, and the Austrian currency was devalued in 1811 due to a massive depression brought on by the Napoleonic Wars, and Prince Kinsky was thrown from his horse in 1812, causing his death shortly thereafter. Prince Lobkowitz went bankrupt and fled Vienna in 1813, but Archduke Rudolph covered the patronage fee each time these things happened.

૭૪ૐ

Beethoven dedicated many of his greatest compositions to Rudolph including two piano concertos, the Fourth and Emperor (the 5th), two of his most popular piano sonatas including **"*Les Adieux*"** and the so-called **"*Hammerklavier*,"** his Violin Sonata opus 96, the Archduke Piano Trio (named for Rudolph), the Missa Solemnis, and the Grosse Fugue.

૭૪ૐ

In 1809, Archduke Rudolph and his entire family were forced to leave Vienna when the French army occupied the city, and Beethoven composed "***Les Adieux***" with that in mind. In a particularly poignant gesture, Beethoven composed the opening movement subtitled "***Das Lebewohl***" ("***The Farewell***"), the second movement subtitled "***Die Abwesenheit***" ("***The Absence***"), while he was in exile, and the final movement subtitled "***Das Wiedersehen***" ("***The Homecoming***") when he returned in 1810. The Missa Solemnis was composed to be played at the enthronement of Archduke Rudolph as Archbishop of Olmütz in 1820. Sadly, this work took Beethoven four years to write, and so it was not completed until 1823.

Prince Razumovsky, the Russian ambassador to the court in Vienna, was also a patron, and he commissioned the Razumovsky String Quartets, op 59. Similarly, Count Oppersdorff was a wealthy Viennese patron of the arts with his own orchestra. He was the person who commissioned the Fourth and the Fifth Symphonies. Beethoven met him at the summer estate of Prince Lichnowsky and was there to witness the altercation between Beethoven and Lichnowsky, interceding to stop Beethoven from breaking a chair over the head of the unfortunate Prince.

Beethoven obviously departed the estate and continued to stay in Silesia at the estate of Oppersdorff where his Second Symphony was performed by the private orchestra in residence there. Oppersdorff commissioned both of his next two symphonies, and their relationship flourished when he paid

Beethoven 500 florins for the exclusive use of the Fourth Symphony for six months. He subsequently commissioned the Fifth Symphony for 500 florins, but Beethoven dedicated the symphony to Count Andrey Razumovsky and Prince Joseph Franz von Lobkowitz, thus ending their professional relationship.

❧ VII ❧
BEETHOVEN, THE PERFORMER

"Music is the one incorporeal entrance into the higher world of knowledge which comprehends mankind, but which mankind cannot comprehend."

— LUDWIG VAN BEETHOVEN

As a performer, Beethoven made his mark quickly in Vienna as an improviser and performer of his own work. His technique was powerful and raw, and he attracted huge crowds to the concerts he organized. One contemporary wrote about his playing that he played

> *"his own works very capriciously, though at times his*
> *sensitivity to tempo change and melodic utterance*
> *was of great beauty."*

Another noted that his

> *"extemporizations were the most extraordinary things that one could hear. No artist I ever heard came at all near the height which Beethoven attained."*

His student and the greatest piano pedagogue in history wrote that Beethoven's

> *"extraordinary extempore playing (i.e., his improvisations) was his greatest gift as a performer,"*

and he noted that in

> *"the rapidity of scale passages, trills, leaps, etc. no one equaled this man."*

⚜

Of course, his hearing began to be an issue in the early years of the 1800s, and he began to refuse offers to perform to keep the rumors of his deafness at bay. He had always been a willful and highly sensitive performer, uncharacteristically refusing to perform if his listeners, who were frequently aristocrats, were talking.

⚜

The piano was, by this time, established as the bourgeois instrument par excellence, and every household of note had one in it. This was because of the changing society in which courts were no longer the sole performance venue. Instead, private and public concerts were popular, and when middle-class patrons attended, they frequently purchased the piano reductions of the works they heard of playing at home. Beethoven knew this and took to performing in these public concerts. He played his music and the Prelude and Fugues of Johann Sebastian Bach's Well Tempered Clavier.

❧

Beethoven's first public performance (meaning not for a private group of aristocrats) was in Vienna in March 1795, a concert in which he first performed one of his piano concertos. It is uncertain whether this was the First or Second. Neither of these concertos was complete at the time, and it is conjectured that he improvised large sections of the piano solo. Shortly after this performance, he arranged for the publication of the first of his compositions to which he assigned an opus number, the three piano trios, Opus 1. These works were dedicated to Prince Lichnowsky and were financially successful; the profits were almost enough to cover his living expenses for a year.

❧ VIII ❧
BEETHOVEN, THE COMPOSER

"Don't only practice your art but force your way into its secrets; art deserves that, for it and knowledge can raise man to the Divine."

— LUDWIG VAN BEETHOVEN

❧

Beethoven was a composer who set the standard for other composers throughout his life. He had a career that was the envy of nearly everyone in Vienna at the time. His musical style was unique and continuously developing, but the constant in his style was the use of the sonata-allegro form. This formed a sort of musical interpretation of the current ideas of dialectical discourse, the new Napoleonic legal system, which provided two opposing sides - the defendant and the plaintiff - to understand the intricacies of complicated cases and the relatively new scientific method (of observation, experimentation, conclusion). In this way, it is a form that is in line with the new ways of thinking about serious topics.

SONATA FORM

❦

The Sonata-allegro form was so-called because it was often used to construct the first movement in a sonata (the quick or '*allegro*' movement). It consisted of two opposing themes (or one theme in two different keys) that were presented in their original form in the first section of the work, called the Exposition. After they have been presented in their original form, a new section is introduced, in which the two themes are manipulated, changed, developed, and otherwise discussed in the section called the Development. Finally, after the musical discussion is finished, (and this was increasingly the longest of the sections), the two themes would be presented for the final time in the section called the Recapitulation, in which the two themes are presented in the last key of the work, thus bringing the musical discussion to a close. Rather than a form in the strict sense of the word, (like the rondo, the various dance forms or themes, and variations) this was a musical process, a means of making music into a discussion.

While Haydn and Mozart are often credited with creating this musical process, it was Beethoven who took it to its apotheosis. Works like the final movement of his Ninth Symphony took the sonata-allegro form to new heights. In many of Beethoven's works, the sonata form was used for many of the movements and in a few select cases, in all the four movements.

The Sonata-Allegro form was the most often used form in Beethoven's music, but he also excelled at the theme and variation form in such works as the Diabelli Variations, a work for piano that took the simple concept of the form to new and daring heights. He was also an expert at reinvigorating older forms. Beethoven was a student of Bach's contrapuntal work and had studied counterpoint longer and more deeply than any composer of his time. Thus, he was adept at the baroque process called the fugue in which themes are intertwined in a very complicated manner that often defied the logic of the listener. His greatest fugue was the work for string quartet that he entitled the "***Grosse Fugue***," meaning the "***Great Fugue***." It was a work of such complexity that when it was first affixed to other movements of a string quartet, it had to be separated because it made the other movements, which were far more complex than any other movements in any other sonata, seem trite.

BEETHOVEN'S STYLE

❧

I t is safe to say that Beethoven made his music greater in every sense than any of his contemporaries, including Mozart who also spent a great deal of time studying the music of Johann Sebastian Bach in his later years. Mozart's Requiem, for example, was a profoundly crafted work of contrapuntal complexity, but it was left unfinished at his death and completed in a very unsatisfying way by his second-rate student, Suessmayr.

❧

For all his studied complexity, Beethoven's creative work can be divided into three distinct periods: the early period, in which he had mastered the Classical style that had been established by Haydn and Mozart; the middle period, often referred to as the Heroic Period, from 1802-1812, in which he was profoundly inspired by the great changes that were going on in the political realm, inspired by the newly created democracies created by the revolutions in the United States (1776) and France (1789); and his Late Period from 1812-1827, in which he went back into the past to incorporate and improve upon the musical styles of the baroque masters. This is the period in which he used the fugue and other baroque forms.

ॐ

His early period, typically considered to have begun in about 1792 and ending in 1802, is characterized by his First two symphonies, his early piano sonatas and his early string quartets. These were works that were squarely within the Classical tradition, adhering to the forms and style that were prevalent and popular at the time. In fact, if Beethoven had died at this time, he would have been remembered as a skilled Classicist, with little of the fire that characterized his later work. The only notable exception to this is the op 13 Piano Sonata, called the "***Pathétique***," from 1799, which, even to observers at the time, seemed out of character with none of the reserves of his earlier work. Even in this early period, his music began to attract the attention of those in the vanguard of musical development.

ॐ

His compositions between 1800 and 1802, still considered as his early period, were dominated by two large-scale orchestral works, although he continued to produce other important works such as the "***Moonlight Sonata***." In the spring of 1801, though he completed music for a ballet called The Creatures of Prometheus, this piece was widely popular and to capitalize on the success, he rushed to produce and publish a piano reduction of the work. Then, in the spring of 1802, he completed his Second Symphony, intended for performance at a concert that was canceled. The symphony received its premiere instead at a subscription concert in April 1803 at the public Theater an der Wien where he had been appointed as a composer in residence. He began to make plans for a grand opera as well to be called (tentatively) Leonore, (which eventually became Fidelio).

※

In addition to the Second Symphony, the concert also featured his First Symphony, the Third Piano Concerto, and the oratorio Christ on the Mount of Olives. This monumental concert, which apparently went on for more than five hours, received mixed reviews but earned him a great deal of money because, on the strength of his reputation, he was able to charge three times the regular fee for a concert.

※

His business dealings with publishers also began to improve in 1802 when his brother, Kaspar, who had previously assisted him casually, started to assume a larger role in his financial management. In addition to negotiating higher prices for recently composed works, Kaspar began selling some of his earlier unpublished compositions and encouraged him (against Beethoven's preference) to also make arrangements and transcriptions of his more popular works for other instrumental combinations. Beethoven only did this menial musical work because he knew that his publishers would have hired second-rate arrangers if he had not done it himself, and Beethoven was always keenly aware of the importance of earning a living as a composer.

Beethoven's Middle Period, often called the Heroic Period (1802-12), was marked by his return from Heiligenstadt and his contemplation of suicide. When he returned, he made a concerted effort to change his musical style, and this resulted in larger scale works like the Third ("*Eroica*") Symphony in E-flat, the most heroic of the keys, according to Beethoven. When it premiered in early 1805, it was received with confusion and excitement in equal parts.

EROICA SYMPHONY

This four-movement symphony was conceived on a grand scale and was originally entitled *"**Bonaparte**"* to be an homage to the great leader of the French Revolution, Napoleon Bonaparte. However, Beethoven was reportedly enraged when Napoleon crowned himself Emperor of France and changed the dedication to Sinfonia Eroica, subtitled *"**to the memory of a great man**."*

The first movement, marked as Allegro con brio, is in a sonata allegro form that contains the most extended development section ever written to that time. In ¾ time, it begins with two large E ♭ major chords, played by the whole orchestra, which establishes the tonality of the movement.

The main theme begins with the '***cellos***,' introducing the first theme quite quietly with a "***wrong note***" inserted (C#) to throw the tonality into question and set the work off in another direction. The melody ends with a statement by the first violins and a syncopated series of Gs. The first theme is then played again by the various instruments.

❦

True to sonata form, the piece then moves to the dominant (V) key of B ♭ , but Beethoven introduces several smaller themes so that the movement contains not two but five themes that are then developed in the next section. The lyrical second theme, the one that is developed in the Development section is not stated until b. 83, which is strangely late for a second theme. The climactic moment of the exposition arrives when the music is interrupted by six consecutive sforzando chords (b. 128–131). Later, and following the concluding chords of the exposition (mm. 144–148), the main theme returns in a brief codetta (m. 148) that transitions into the development.

❦

The Development section had a high number of strange forays into unrelated keys. Typically, this is the job of the development section, but Beethoven takes this idea to a new level. With syncopated rhythms and loud statements of seemingly unrelated material, the section is confusing to a first-time listener. The frequent statements of crashing sforzando chords have been interpreted as outbursts of rage by many observers. After the statements of the various themes, there is a new theme introduced in E minor, a very distant key, which nearly doubles the length of the development section and confuses the accepted formula of the classical sonata, which precludes new material in the development section.

☙❧

It is worth noting that Beethoven's scores were notoriously messy, and so copyists frequently made errors in the transcription. It was believed that the French horn part was written incorrectly for many years because of the strangeness of the passage and for its apparent disconnection from the rest of the piece.

☙❧

The recapitulation section, rather than simply stating the principal themes again in the tonic (E flat) key, has a sudden excursion into F major. Following this, the work resumes the predictable form of a recapitulation. The movement ends in a long coda that reintroduces the new theme first presented in the development section.

☙❧

The second movement, marked by Marcia funebre - adagio assai, is a funeral march in ternary (A-B-A) form. This means that the original subject is stated at the beginning and the end of the work with a secondary subject in the middle. In the sad relative minor key of C minor, it begins with the march theme played by the strings and then by the woodwinds. A second theme in the relative major of E ♭.

☙❧

The middle (B) section of the funeral march is in C major, a strangely funny key. Rather than a simple restatement of the first theme (in a Haydn work, for example, he would not even bother to write out the music, indicating a repeat), Beethoven states the C minor theme again and then creates a fugue in the related key of F minor based on an inversion of the original second theme. The first theme is restated in the dominant (G minor) followed by a somewhat tumultuous development section that followed by a full re-statement of the first theme and announced by the plaintive oboe. Then a short coda is stated taken from the major key section of the B section and eventually concludes with a quiet statement of the main theme that seems to crumble into short fragments interspersed with unexplained silences.

🙦🙧

Typically, the third movement would be a dance called a minuet. Beethoven, though, sped up the minuet to Allegro vivace, which is in the scherzo (or playful) tempo marking, in B ♭ that sounds like a chase between several similar musical elements. It is short and intensely exciting. Normally, with a minuet, there is a section between the two statements of the dance theme, in which the strings take a break, and the woodwinds and brass get a chance to shine. This is called the trio, and so the *__minuet and trio__* became a standard, but light part of a symphony. Beethoven takes this idea and makes it into a monumental element, with three French horns playing the melody, a first in the classical symphony. The scherzo is then restated in an abbreviated form followed by a coda that gradually builds in volume until it ends in a huge fortissimo crash.

🙦🙧

The final movement, also marked Allegro molto because of its high intensity, is a theme and ten variations on a bass line (this is often referred to as a passacaglia). The variations are incredibly original, including teo fugues (variation 4 and 7), and introducing new musical material in variation 3. The ending of the movement is huge -- it seems to sum up the entire meaning of the word heroic and brilliantly ends the symphony back in its home key of E ♭ .

CONCLUSION

❧

The "*middle period*" of Beethoven's life is often associated with a "*heroic*" manner of composing, and it is appropriate in some cases, and in others like the Pastoral (6th) Symphony, it is not. What characterizes this period the most is an extending of the given parameters of the musical style of Haydn and Mozart, using complicated and brilliant harmonies, instrumental combinations, and musical language. This middle period includes the symphonies from the Third (the Eroica just discussed) up to the Eighth Symphony, but also the middle period string quartets and the "*Waldstein*" and "*Appassionata*" piano sonatas. It also includes his only opera, Fidelio, his Violin Concerto and his oratorio Christ on the Mount of Olives.

❧

This period of his life was the time when he confronted his deafness with an extraordinary burst of creative energy, and when he had earned a great deal of money from the sale of this music to publishers. He had a contract as a composer in residence with the Theater an der Wien, which was canceled when the theatre changed management in 1804. This put a great deal of trouble for Beethoven who was trying to write Fidelio (then called Leonore) and forced him to move to cheaper housing with a friend. When Fidelio finally opened in 1805, to Beethoven's surprise, it was greeted with very little enthusiasm. It was a "*rescue*" opera, in which a nobleman is falsely imprisoned and rescued by his true love, the heroine Leonore. The houses were empty not because of the quality of the opera, but because the French troops were occupying Vienna at the time and people were not favorably disposed to going out in the evenings. Beethoven, though, took this as a criticism and began trying to fix it. It never was a huge success and remained as the notable weakness in Beethoven's oeuvre.

۞

Nevertheless, this work was one of the central pillars of Beethoven's middle period work. The writer, E. T. A. Hoffmann, called him one of the three great "*Romantic*" composers together with Haydn and Mozart. Although these composers tend to be associated with the Classical period nowadays, the use of the term "*Romantic*" for the music of the early nineteenth century has since come to be generally accepted. Thus, Beethoven is often regarded as a Classical composer as well as a Romantic composer.

BEETHOVEN'S LATE PERIOD

❧

Beethoven's late period (1812-27) is generally formed by an intense study of the work of the baroque masters, Bach, Handel, and Vivaldi, which were being redis-covered and published at around 1812. It was stylistically char-acterized by increased complexity and use of counterpoint and the forms that were common in the baroque period (1600-1750).

❧

His work that is generally regarded as the first work of his late period is Wellington's Victory, a graphic depiction of the Battle of Waterloo, Napoleon's final battle. This work, gener-ally not regarded as one of his great works, was considered by Beethoven to be his favorite piece of music. He incorporated *"The Marseillaise,"* *"British Grenadiers*," and *"Rule Britannia"* as musical material. Originally entitled The Battle Symphony, Beethoven considered it as a symphony, but

Beethoven scholars have been loath to include it in the list of his symphonies because of its quality.

۞

More in the style of his late works were the first piano sonatas he had written in five years, op. 27, markedly more romantic in style than any of his previous sonatas (this includes the so-called "***Moonlight***" sonata, op. 267, #2), and his song cycle An die ferne Geliebte (1816), which is generally considered to be the first song cycle, ancestor to the great works by Schubert and Schumann.

۞

Up to this point, from 1812-1816, he wrote relatively few works because of the drama that was going on in his personal life surrounding his nephew and his deafness. But he had a renewal of his output in 1816, thanks to the patriotic music he supplied surrounding the Congress of Vienna, headed by the great statesman Klemens Metternich, to settle the long-term peace of Europe after the Napoleonic Wars. However, after this burst of energy, he again wrote relatively little until 1818 when he experienced another burst of creative energy.

۞

He returned to piano compositions, which included his last five sonatas (including the Hammerklavier) and his massive Diabelli Variations. Other works of his late period include the last two sonatas for cello and piano, the late string quartets, and two large-scale works, the Ninth Symphony (originally planned as two separate symphonies) and his mass, the Missa Solemnis.

The Diabelli Variations was started as part of a competition to write the best set of keyboard variations on a theme supplied by the composer and publisher, Anton Diabelli, to what he believed were the greatest composers of Austria, to write one variation each. Beethoven, at first, refused because he considered that the supplied music to be banal, but upon learning that Diabelli was willing to pay well for this, he decided to see how good he could make this trite theme. The result is generally considered the most magnificent set of variations ever conceived.

He had been sketching out his Missa Solemnis, but he set it aside to concentrate on what he thought would be a cash cow. This set of thirty-three variations took him until 1823 and was supposedly inspired by the set of forty variations composed by Archduke Rudolph on a theme by Beethoven himself. The Diabelli Variations includes almost every form then in use, including a fugetta and a grand fugue.

For the next few years, he continued to work on the Missa Solemnis, composing piano sonatas and bagatelles to satisfy the demands of publishers and the need for income. He was not healthy at this time and became seriously ill in 1821, but recovered and resumed his composing of the Missa Solemnis, originally planned to be performed in 1819.

Beethoven was highly regarded at this time that the composer Peters was planning complete works of Beethoven. This plan was finally completed in 1971! However, his brother, Johann, began to take over his business affairs, negotiating successfully with publishers for good rates on his many smaller compositions and older unpublished works. Beethoven was amassing a fortune during this period.

∞❧∞

In 1822, Beethoven received two commissions that would result in two of his greatest works. The Philharmonic Society of London offered a commission for one symphony, and a Russian Prince named Nikolas Golitsin of St. Petersburg offered to pay Beethoven's very high fee for three string quartets. The commission from the Philharmonic Society resulted in his finishing the Ninth Symphony, which was premiered along with the Missa Solemnis on 7 May 1824 to great acclaim at the Kärntnertor Theater under his own baton. The Allgemeine musikalische Zeitung wrote of this concert that Beethoven's

"inexhaustible genius had shown us a new world."

∞❧∞

Despite the critical success of this concert, it did not make him as much as he had anticipated. The second concert on 24 May, in which the producer guaranteed Beethoven a minimum fee, was not well attended; nephew Karl noted that

"many people [had] already gone into the country."

It was Beethoven's last public concert.

Beethoven then turned to write the string quartets for Golitsin. This series of works, now known as the "***Late Quartets***," went beyond what musicians or audiences were ready for at that time. Although when they were premiered, few listeners understood them, and opinion has changed considerably. These works are now considered as some of the most advanced music of the entire nineteenth century. Beethoven's favorite string quartets was the Fourteenth, op. 131 in C♯ minor, which he commented that he considered it his single perfect composition.

Beethoven wrote the last quartets while in very bad health. From April 1825, he was bedridden for a month. His recovery from illness is the inspiration for the slow movement of the Fifteenth Quartet, which he called "***Holy song of thanks ('Heiliger Dankgesang') to the divinity, from one made-well***." Nevertheless, he went on to complete the quartets now numbered Thirteenth, Fourteenth, and Sixteenth. The last work Beethoven wrote was the final replacement movement of the Thirteenth Quartet, which replaced the Große Fugue which now stands on its own. Very shortly afterward, in December 1826, he became ill again.

❧ IX ❧
DEAFNESS AND THE HEILIGENSTADT TESTAMENT

"Music should strike fire from the heart of man and bring tears from the eyes of woman."

— LUDWIG VAN BEETHOVEN

❧

One of the worst possible afflictions to affect a musician is deafness. When Beethoven was only twenty-six years old, he began to experience ringing in his ears. He reported this to his friends back in Bonn but did not report it to any of his closest friends. He was keenly aware of the stigma that would affect him if it got out that he was going deaf, and particularly since he was not only a composer but a noted performer as well. In fact, according to contemporary reports, he was the best pianist anyone had ever seen, and so being deaf would make his performing career severely curtailed.

By 1801, his hearing had deteriorated to such an extent that he could not interact in public. He wrote in a letter at that time:

> *"... it is curious that in conversation, there are people who do not notice my condition at all; since I have generally been absent-minded, they account for it in that way. Often I can scarcely hear someone speaking softly, the tones yes, but not the words. However, as soon as anyone shouts, it becomes intolerable..."*

To some extent, his deafness remains a mystery to many. Some researchers point to the large amount of lead in his system, presumably taken from the lead plates that he ate off of unwittingly. Other theories suggest that he may have contracted typhus or syphilis, which may have affected his hearing. Another theory suggests that it was caused by his habit of immersing his head in cold water to stay awake. The truth is nobody knows exactly what was wrong with him, other than it seems to have been a severe tinnitus. There were days when he was able to hear things right up until 1816, but other days, he was stone deaf.

In 1802, Beethoven considered suicide because it was so worrisome to him. He took a short vacation to a small town called Heiligenstadt where he wrote a testament that convinced him to keep fighting that his disability was less potent than his drive to succeed.

> *"...for six years now, I have been hopelessly afflicted, made worse by senseless physicians, from year to year, deceived with hopes of improvement, finally compelled to face the prospect of a lasting malady (whose cure will take years or, perhaps, be impossible). Though born with a fiery active temperament, even susceptible to the diversions of society, I was soon compelled to isolate myself to live life alone. If, at times, I tried to forget all this, oh how harshly was I flung back by the doubly sad experience of my bad hearing. Yet, it was impossible for me to say to people, "Speak louder, shout, for I am deaf.""*

๑๛๛

This sad statement was only part of a long document in which he considered but eventually rejected suicide. He continued:

> *"Ah, how could I possibly admit an infirmity in the one sense which ought to be more perfect in me than others, a sense which I once possessed in the highest perfection, a perfection such as few in my profession enjoys or ever has enjoyed. Oh, I cannot do it; therefore, forgive me when you see me draw back when I would have gladly mingled with you. My misfortune is doubly painful to me because I am bound to be misunderstood; for me, there can be no relaxation with my fellow men,*

no refined conversations, no mutual exchange of ideas. I must live almost alone, like one who has been banished; I can mix with society only as much as true necessity demands. If I approach near to people, a hot terror seizes upon me, and I fear being exposed to the danger that my condition might be noticed. Thus, it has been during the last six months, which I have spent in the country. By ordering me to spare my hearing as much as possible, my intelligent doctor almost fell in with my own present frame of mind, though, sometimes I ran counter to it by yielding to my desire for companionship. But what a humiliation for me when someone standing next to me heard a flute in the distance, and I heard nothing, or someone standing next to me heard a shepherd singing, and again, I heard nothing. Such incidents drove me almost to despair; a little more of that, and I would have ended my life. It was only my art that held me back."

◈

This statement of hopelessness was mitigated by his fervent desire to create art for the world, the world that had seemingly abandoned him. A singularly impatient composer chose patience:

"Patience, they say, is what I must now choose for my guide, and I have done so.... Perhaps I shall get better, perhaps not; I am ready. - Forced to become a philosopher already in my twenty-eighth year, - oh, it is not easy, and for the artist, much more difficult than for anyone else. ...Oh, fellow men,

when at some point you read this, consider then that you have done me an injustice; someone who has had misfortune man console himself to find a similar case to his, who, despite all the limitations of Nature, nevertheless did everything within his powers to become accepted among worthy artists and men. - You, my brothers, Carl, and [Johann], as soon as I am dead, if Dr. Schmid is still alive, ask him in my name to describe my malady, and attach this written documentation to his account of my illness so that so far as it is possible, at least the world may become reconciled to me after my death. - At the same time, I declare you two to be the heirs to my small fortune (if so it can be called); divide it fairly; bear with and help each other. What injury you have done me, you know was long ago forgiven. To you, brother Carl, I give special thanks for the attachment you have shown me of late. It is my wish that you may have a better and freer life than I have had. Recommend virtue to your children; it alone, not money, can make them happy. I speak from experience; this was what upheld me in time of misery. Thanks to it and to my art, I did not end my life by suicide. - Farewell and love each other. - I thank all my friends, particularly Prince Lichnowsky and Professor Schmid. - I would like the instruments from Prince L. to be preserved by one of you, but not to be the cause of strife between you, and as soon as they can serve you a better purpose, then sell them. How happy I shall be if can still be helpful to you in my grave, - so be it. - With joy, I hasten towards death. - If it comes before I have had the chance to develop all my artistic capacities, it will still be coming too soon despite my harsh fate, and I should probably wish it later. - Yet, even so, I should be happy, for would it not free me from a state of endless suffering? - Come when thou wilt, I shall meet thee bravely. - Farewell and do not wholly forget me when I am dead; I deserve this from you, for during my lifetime, I was thinking of you often and of ways to make you happy - be so."

— LUDWIG VAN BEETHOVEN

— HEILIGENSTADT,

— OCTOBER 6TH, 1802

৩৯৩

This singular and unique view into the soul of Beethoven has been a boon to historians, but it reveals the torture that had seized the composer at the height of his musical and creative powers. As we now know, he clearly chose to live with his affliction - deafness - and to strive to outdo his previous work. Beethoven had a piano fitted with an iron bar attached to the sounding board that he bit to feel the vibrations that he could not hear, thus allowing him to experience some semblance of what music sounded like.

৩৯৩

It is now known that he never recovered from this deafness, and although he continued in a limited way to perform, he was clearly affected by his malady. In private conversations, we are fortunate to have records of many of his conversations because the interlocutor would have to write down questions and statements in what are now known as the conversation books. These reveal a great deal of the inner workings of the man's brain and provide us with a glimpse into the emotions, thoughts, feelings, and ideas of the great deaf composer.

❦ X ❦

BEETHOVEN'S LEGACY

"Music is the mediator between the spiritual and the sensual life."

— LUDWIG VAN BEETHOVEN

❦

Beethoven is now remembered as the composer who, in many ways, was the progenitor of the Romantic style. Most composers who came after him agreed that they could not compare themselves to him. Brahms was so affected by the music of Beethoven that he dared not write a symphony until he felt he could master all of Beethoven's style. Mahler was deathly afraid of beginning his Tenth Symphony because, through the nineteenth century, there developed a superstition that this would lead to one's death. In fact, Mahler did die shortly thereafter. Wagner revered Beethoven as the greatest of the German composers and held him as the standard to which all German composers must strive. He tried things that had never occurred to anyone before, like the choral symphony, his Ninth. Beethoven was also responsible for adding many instruments to the modern orchestra. Before his time, horns were only occasionally used in orchestras, and piccolos, english horns, and contra-bassoons were new additions. He was the acknowledged master of the development method of composition, developing musical lines and melodies from germs of ideas that were worked out in the process of the piece's unfolding. In fact, Beethoven was the main inspiration for the new trends in twentieth-century music; his works and his way of living became the standard of the suffering artist. It is undeniable that he suffered from his failed love affairs and his deafness that caused him great distress through his life, which was reflected in his music.

෬෨

Beethoven left a wealth of secondary material, including his sketches for his works, his conversation notebooks, and many other writings that have kept scholars busy for hundreds of years.

❧ XI ❧

THE IMMORTAL
BELOVED

"Music is a higher revelation than all wisdom and philosophy."

— LUDWIG VAN BEETHOVEN

※

One of the greatest mysteries in the study of Beethoven is the identity of the immortal beloved. Beethoven wrote this letter at some point in his life, but apparently, he never mailed it. It was found among his papers when he died in 1827:

(Monday) 6 July, morning.

> *"My angel, my all, my own self — only a few words*
> *today, and that too with pencil (with yours) —*
> *only till tomorrow is my lodging definitely fixed.*

What abominable waste of time in such things —
why this deep grief where necessity speaks?

Can our love persist otherwise than through sacrifices
than by not demanding everything? Can you
change it that you are not entirely mine, I not
entirely yours? Oh, God, look into beautiful
Nature and compose your mind to the inevitable.
Love demands everything and is quite right, so it
is for me with you, for you with me — only you
forget so easily, that I must live for you and for
me — if we were quite united, you would notice
this painful feeling as little as I should.

We will probably soon meet, even today, I cannot
communicate my remarks to you, which, during
these days, I made about my life — if only our
hearts were close together, I would probably not
make any remarks like this. My heart is full, to
tell you much — there are moments when I find
that speech is nothing at all. Brighten up —
remain my true and only treasure, my all, as I to
you. The rest the gods must send, what must be
for us and will.
Your faithful
Ludwig"

৩৩

Monday evening, 6 July

"You suffer, you, my dearest creature. Just now I
noticed that letters must be mailed first thing
early. Mondays — Thursdays — the only days,

when the post goes from here to K. You suffer —
oh! Where I am, you are with me, with me and
you, I will arrange that I may live with you.
What a life!

So! Without you — pursued by the kindness of the
people here and there, whom I mean — to want
to earn just as little as they earn — humility of
man towards men — it pains me — and when I
regard myself in connection with the Universe,
what I am, and what he is — whom one calls the
greatest — and yet — there lies here again the
godlike of man. I weep when I think you will
probably only receive on Saturday the first news
from me — as you too love — yet I love you
stronger — but never hide yourself from me.
Good night — as I am taking the waters, I must
go to bed. Oh God — so near! So far! Is it not a
real building of heaven, our Love — but as firm,
too, as the citadel of heaven?"

৩১৫৩

Good morning, on (Tuesday) 7 July

"Even in bed, my ideas yearn towards you, my
Immortal Beloved, here and there joyfully, then
again sadly, awaiting from Fate, whether it will
listen to us. I can only live, either altogether with
you or not at all. Yes, I have determined to
wander about for so long far away, until I can fly
into your arms and call myself quite at home with
you, can send my soul enveloped by yours into the
realm of spirits — Yes, I regret, it must be. You

*will get over it all the more as you know my
faithfulness to you; never another one can own
my heart, never — never! O God, why must one
go away from what one loves so, and yet my life
in W. As it is now is a miserable life. Your love
made me the happiest and unhappiest at the same
time. At my actual age, I should need some
continuity, sameness of life — can that exist under
our circumstances? Angel, I just heard that the
post goes out every day — and must close,
therefore, so that you get the L. at once. Be calm
— love me — today — yesterday.*

*What longing in tears for you — You — my Life —
my All — farewell. Oh, go on loving me — never
doubt the faithfullest heart*

*Of your beloved
L
Ever yours.
Ever mine.
Ever ours."*

❧

It seems that these letters were sent from Teplitz, a spa town
in the area, which is the modern Czech Republic in July of
1812 (judging by the dates and days and the watermark on the
paper), but the identity of the "***immortal beloved***" has never
been adequately explained. Perhaps it was Antonie Brentano,
the sister-in-law of Bettina Brentano, the lover of Goethe.
Antonie had been living in Vienna, away from her husband,
taking care of her father's estate and met Beethoven in 1812.
This is the theory proposed by scholar Maynard Solomon in

1972, but it has been contested by many scholars since because Beethoven was friends with Franz Brentano, and Beethoven had a strict code of ethics that would have precluded an affair with a married woman, especially one married to his friend.

ᗧ•••ᗢ

Another theory was that the "***immortal beloved***" was Countess Terez von Brunsvik, one of Beethoven's students and a distinguished member of the nobility who is credited with the founding of the first "***Kindergarten***." A more likely candidate, according to Beethoven scholars, is her sister, Josephine von Brunsvik, who was also one of his students from 1899. According to Beethoven, she was "***enthusiastic***" about their relationship and even he felt that he had to suppress his feelings for her. Their relationship developed over many years, much to the consternation of her widowed mother who was keen to marry her daughters to wealthy noblemen, and Beethoven was decidedly not noble. To the intensely class-conscious Austrian nobility, this was an impossibility, and Beethoven, an iconoclast by any standard, who refused to wear a wig and was slovenly in his dress, critical of the nobility, and dismissive of social convention.

ᗧ•••ᗢ

Countess Josephine von Brunsvik married the much older Count Joseph Daym and bore him three children. She was pregnant with a fourth child in 1804 when he died (he was much older than her). Beethoven was a frequent visitor to the household, and this continued even after she was widowed. The family put a great deal of pressure on her to end the relationship, and she complied after 1807. She went on a long trip to find a suitable teacher for her school-aged children, and when the famous educator, Johann Heinrich Pestalozzi, recommended the Estonian Baron Christoph von Stackelberg, they went to meet with him. Although Josephine was ill, Stackelberg apparently forced himself on her and impregnated her, thereby forcing a marriage that was seen as scandalous and unhappy.

❦

In 1812, they agreed to continue only as a platonic, and when Stackelberg bought an expensive estate that ruined them, he left her. Her life got worse and worse, but in 1812, she may have returned to Beethoven's constant love for her.

❦

Other candidates who have been conjectured with various degrees of mainstream scholarly support are Julie (*"**Giulietta**"*) Guicciardi, who was a cousin to the Brunsvik sisters. Beethoven took Julie (as she was called) as a student in 1801, and he wrote to his friend Franz Wegeler:

> *"My life is once more a little more pleasant, I'm out and about again, among people – you can hardly believe how desolate, how sad my life has been since these last two years; this change was caused by a sweet, enchanting girl, who loves me and whom I love. After two years, I am again enjoying some moments of bliss, and it is the first time that – I feel that marriage could make me happy, but unfortunately, she is not of my station – and now – I certainly could not marry now."*

In 1823, he confessed to Anton Schindler, his secretary and first biographer that he was indeed in love with her. Countess Theresa Brunsvik believed that the letters were to Josephine and said so publicly, casting doubt on Schindler's claim.

◌⁙◌

Amalie Sebald was a young German singer whom Beethoven met at Teplitz in 1812 while he was taking the waters there. Apparently he was quite taken with her, but it is doubtful if he would have written these letters to her when she was actually with him.

◌⁙◌

Dorothea von Ertmann was a pianist whom Beethoven knew. Although she was married, he was very interested in her, calling her his Dorothea-Cecilia. She premiered several of his pieces, and he was known to have comforted her after her only child died in 1804. She established a salon dedicated to the work of Beethoven and Schindler credited her with keeping Beethoven's music fashionable.

◌⁙◌

Therese Malfatti was a pianist and the dedicatee of the famous Fur Elise bagatelle that has become one of Beethoven's best-known works. Beethoven was in love with her in 1810 and wrote a now-famous letter to her that read, in part:

> "Now fare you well, respected Therese. I wish you all
> the good and beautiful things of this life. Bear me

in memory—no one can wish you a brighter,
happier life than I—even should it be that you
care not at all for
Your devoted servant and friend, Beethoven."

ॐ

Marie von Erdödy met Beethoven in 1804. Born in 1779 and married at 17, Countess Anna Maria von Erdödy separated from her husband and lived in Vienna. An accomplished pianist, she held musical soirées at her Vienna apartment. By 1808, Beethoven was actively considering leaving Vienna. Countess von Erdödy was instrumental in establishing an alliance between Prince Lobkowitz, Prince Kinsky, and Archduke Rudolph that resulted in Beethoven being given an annual salary of 4,000 florins if he agreed to reside permanently in Vienna. Beethoven agreed and stayed in Vienna for the remainder of his life. To express his gratitude for her part in this arrangement, Beethoven wrote and dedicated the two piano trios to the Countess.

ॐ

Finally, Bettina von Arnim, nee Brentano, was a writer, publisher, composer, singer, visual artist, illustrator, patron of young talent, and a social activist. She was the archetype of the Romantic era's zeitgeist and the crux of many creative relationships of canonical artistic figures. Best known for the company she kept, she was close friends with Goethe and Beethoven. Many leading composers of the time, including Robert Schumann, Franz Liszt, Johanna Kinkel, and Johannes Brahms, admired her spirit and talents. As a composer, her style was unique, using folk melodies and historical themes combined with innovative harmonies, phrase lengths, and improvisations that became synonymous with the music of the era. She was married to Achim von Arnim. She was a formidable woman but not the likely subject of the letters.

⚜

Ultimately, nobody knows exactly who the recipient of the letters, which were either not mailed or sent back to Beethoven, was. What we can glean from them was that Beethoven was a very romantic lover, although quite likely his love was unrequited.

XII

HOW CAN WE USE BEETHOVEN IN CONTEMPORARY LIFE?

Beethoven is a difficult figure in musical history; while he was a profoundly dedicated composer, he was also dedicated to enriching himself with his work. And while he was a great composer, he was a difficult person to get along with, alienating many, including wealthy patrons. He was such a great composer though he was often forgiven for his outbursts. This image, as the composer and an iconoclast has endured until the present day. While his life was no model for any composer, his compositional rigor is the envy of almost any contemporary composer, and his unique sense of self, as different and better by virtue of his work, has been the model for artists from Picasso to Andy Warhol, from Brahms to Mauricio Kagel, from Browning to T. S. Eliot. The artist, as seen by modern western society, was largely created by the myth of Beethoven as a lonely genius, toiling in pain and isolation from the unforgiving and un-understanding world.

❧ XIII ❧
FURTHER READING

❦

- Solomon, Maynard, Beethoven, New York, Schirmer, 2001
- Lockwood, Lewis, Beethoven: The Music and the Life, New York: Norton, 2002
- Kerman, Joseph; Tyson, Alan; Drabkin, William; Johnson, Douglas; The New Grove Beethoven, New York: Norton, 1983

YOUR FREE EBOOK!

As a way of saying thank you for reading our book, we're offering you a free copy of the below eBook.

Happy Reading!

GO WWW.THEHISTORYHOUR.COM/CLEO/

Made in the USA
Monee, IL
07 June 2021

70547571R00049